SCHOLASTIC

READ-ALOUD PLAYS

CIVIL RIGHTS

New York • Toronto • London • Auckland • Sydney
Mexico City • New Delhi • Hong Kong • Buenos Aires

Teaching Resources

This book is dedicated to every person
who was (and is) committed
to the fight for civil rights.

"Jackie Robinson: Most Valuable Player" originally appeared in *Scholastic Scope*, September 22, 1995; "Martin Luther King, Jr.: Dreams of Justice" originally appeared in *Scholastic Scope*, January 8, 2001; "The Rosa Parks Story" originally appeared in *Scholastic Scope*, February 25, 2002; "Thurgood Marshall: The Fight for Equal Justice," and "Shirley Chisholm: Unbought and Unbossed" originally appeared in *African Americans Who Made a Difference*, Scholastic, 1996.

Cover design by Josué Castilleja
Interior design by Maria Lilja
Interior illustrations by Teresa Southwell

1 2 3 4 5 6 7 8 9 10   40   10   09 08 07 06 05 04

Contents

Introduction

Welcome to this engaging glimpse into a critical era of U.S. history. In *Read-Aloud Plays: Civil Rights*, you will find an intimate look at five inspiring men and women who had a direct impact on the civil rights movement. The plays that follow will enable your students to bear witness to the struggle, pain, grace, and ultimate triumph of these great achievers. For example, baseball great Jackie Robinson withstood the slurs of angry fans and fellow players to forever dismantle the color barrier in professional sports. Rosa Parks refused to budge from a bus seat in Birmingham, Alabama, paving the way for an end to segregation. And while students will read about five remarkable people, we must not forget that their histories represent but a few drops in the deep well of African-American experience. The African-American community is filled with myriad unsung heroes—men and women whose lives would certainly qualify for dramatic chronicle and celebration, if we only knew their stories. It is our hope that these plays serve to broaden student awareness not only of the important role of African Americans in U.S. history as a whole but also the depth of the struggle for civil rights in particular.

The Benefits of Read-Aloud Plays

These plays serve to motivate students at every reading level. Whether students believe that learning history is dull and adds no meaning to their lives, or they are struggling and discouraged readers, the following plays are a surefire way to keep the whole class interested and on task. Read-aloud plays benefit students by:

- building content-area background knowledge.

- exposing kids to content-area vocabulary.

- providing multiple opportunities to read aloud for important fluency practice.

- giving struggling readers small, manageable amounts of text to read.

- fine-tuning students' observational, listening, and oral literacy skills.

- adding variety to an academic routine.

- drawing out quiet or at-risk students.

- encouraging critical thinking and increasing comprehension with background information, fun and creative extension activities, thought-provoking discussion questions, and writing prompts.

How to Use This Book

Feel free to tailor the presentation of these plays to fit your own classroom needs. As they are designed to enrich your existing civil rights curriculum, we suggest using any or all of these plays to kick off or wrap up a civil rights unit. These plays can be "performed" in a variety of ways—from simply reading aloud to staging a production. Whichever way you choose, every student should be encouraged to take on a role and participate in the cooperative effort of the group.

Every effort has been made to have many characters in each play, including important characters for both boys and girls. However, try not to feel limited by traditional roles; rotate roles so that everyone has a chance to appear in a play. This can be a great way to spawn discussion. Girls may protest that they can't play male roles; boys may resist female roles. Although race and gender are often specific and important in the events described, they don't matter in the casting of the plays. In fact, playing characters very different from themselves may deepen students' insight into the times, as well as the events depicted, forging a connection between students and their heritage.

As you go through the school year and students become familiar with the format of the plays, you may find that they want to put on more elaborate productions involving props, scenery, costumes, lighting, and even promotion, tickets, and audiences. Students may want to tinker with a play's content by editing or adding new scenes. Encouraging kids to make these plays their own will only enhance their learning

TIPS

- Many of the plays are divided into two or more scenes. To make sure as many students get a chance to speak as possible, assign new roles each time the scene changes.

- Scan through the play for any unfamiliar vocabulary words to share with students so they won't stumble over them while reading.

- Divide the class into small groups and have each group read the play aloud. Then reassemble the class for a post-play discussion.

- Assign the plays as homework, encouraging students to read the play aloud with family members.

- Use the plays during months celebrating African-American or Women's history.

- Use the plays in conjunction with their related activities will help your students meet many of the English Language Arts and Social Studies standards.

experience. Performing the plays can often bring in students who are shy or uncertain about their reading ability. These students can be instrumental in designing sets and costumes, directing, creating sound effects, and making programs Let students suggest places in the plays where nonspeaking roles can be enlarged or added. These players can work together to pantomime action when they are onstage. However, it is important to encourage reluctant readers to actually read. Practice is essential for their fluency development.

How to Begin

Before distributing each reproducible play, hold a brief discussion to find out what students already know about the historical figure. Consider making available additional books such as those listed in each teaching guide. Share the historical background of the event (also found in the teaching guide) to provide students with a context. You may want to try using the two reading strategies that follow.

PREVIEWING: Because the plays are tailored for a wide audience, you and your students may find it helpful to preview the play to cull a vocabulary list from the text. Read through the cast of characters and their descriptions to familiarize students with the way each name is pronounced. You might also encourage students to spend a few moments acquainting themselves with the characters they are playing by reading over their specific lines. Invite students to ask questions about anything they don't understand. Or, if they think they have a better way to say something, let them experiment with changing the dialogue.

PREDICTING: To enhance comprehension—and enjoyment—before reading the play in class, ask each student to find, as homework, one fact about the subject of the play. Then have them each bring their facts into class for discussion. This will give students something to listen for as they read the play.

Using the Teaching Guide

Following each play is a teaching guide. This section includes background information; activities designed to strengthen students' oral, writing, and researching skills; and book links, as well as several quotes of the historical figures that can be used as prompts for discussion or writing. Encourage students to work cooperatively on many of these activities, and to share their work with the rest of the class.

Additional Resources

Brain Quest: Black History by Barbara C. Ellis (Workman, 2001)

Freedom's Children: Young Civil Rights Activists Tell Their Own Story by Ellen Levine (Sagebrush, 2000)

Internet Scavenger Hunts: Famous Americans by Mela Ottaiano (Scholastic, 2002)

Oh, Freedom: Kids Talk About the Civil Rights Movement With the People Who made It Happen by Casey King and Linda Barrett Osborne (Random House, 1997)

Primary Sources Teaching Kit: Civil Rights by Karen Baiker (Scholastic, 2003)

Jackie Robinson
Most Valuable Player

by Adam Grant

 **Characters**

Narrators 1 and 2

Jackie Robinson

Rachel Robinson,
Jackie's wife

Teammates 1 and 2

Attendant

Scout

Counterman

Branch Rickey,
*President of the
Brooklyn Dodgers*

Bus Driver

Frank Simms,
a journalist

Wendell Smith,
a journalist

Billy Rowe,
a journalist

Clay Hopper,
*Manager of the
Montreal Royals*

Sheriff

Announcer

Eddie Stanky,
a teammate

Newspaper

SCENE 1

NARRATOR 1:   In the spring of 1945, a young man named Jackie Robinson became the shortstop of the Kansas City Monarchs, one of the Negro baseball leagues' top teams. The men who played on teams in the Negro leagues led difficult lives.

NARRATOR 2:   Traveling much of the time in the South, they suffered from the region's terrible Jim Crow laws. Negro leaguers also made much less money than white baseball players. For some players, this was just part of life, but not for Jackie.

NARRATOR 1:   He felt that nothing short of total equality was acceptable for any people, and he fought for his ideals every day, even on the team bus, traveling from game to game.

JACKIE: You fellas had better get ready, because one day, they're going to bring one of us up to the majors. I'm telling you now.

TEAMMATE 1:   Forget it, rookie. It ain't never gonna happen.

NARRATOR 2:   A few minutes later, the bus pulled off the road.

JACKIE: Why are we stopping here?

TEAMMATE 2:   We need gas. And we have to get it here.

JACKIE: Why this gas station?

TEAMMATE 1:   Most places around here won't even serve us. So we gotta fill the extra tanks here. Don't wanna get caught out there somewhere with no gas and nowhere to get it.

NARRATOR 1:   Jackie got off the bus.

JACKIE: Hey, attendant, where's your restroom?

ATTENDANT: Uh, we ain't got one.

JACKIE: You don't have a restroom?

ATTENDANT: Well, we have one, but it's for whites only.

JACKIE:	Okay, we'll get our gas somewhere else, then.
ATTENDANT:	What? You can't do that! You guys always buy one hundred gallons of gas here. We have a deal.
JACKIE:	Now here's the new deal. We all use the restroom, or we don't buy any gas. You got that?
ATTENDANT:	All right, go ahead. But don't tell anybody.
NARRATOR 2:	When the team got back on the bus, they all held their heads a little higher.
JACKIE:	It's a small victory, but it makes a difference.

SCENE 2

NARRATOR 1:	As the season progressed, there were more and more rumors that someone from the Negro leagues might be brought up to the majors. African-American newspapers and lobby groups were carefully keeping the issue constantly in the news.
NARRATOR 2:	Sometimes at the ballpark, Jackie would see a tall, lanky white man in the stands. He seemed to be watching Jackie, scouting him.
TEAMMATE 2:	Hey Jack, who is that guy? He was watching you in Chicago last week. What's up?
JACKIE:	I don't know, I've never seen him before.
NARRATOR 1:	After one game, the man approached Jackie.
SCOUT:	I work for Branch Rickey of the Brooklyn Dodgers. Mr. Rickey asked me to come down and watch you play.
JACKIE:	Pleased to meet you. But what does Rickey want with me?
SCOUT:	He has a few things in mind, maybe starting a Negro league team in Brooklyn. I'd like you to come to New York and meet Mr. Rickey.
NARRATOR 2:	Later, Jackie told his girlfriend Rachel about the meeting.

RACHEL:	Oh Jack. He probably wants you to play for the Dodgers.
JACKIE:	No, I don't think so. I'm beginning to wonder if they're ever going to integrate baseball. There's so much resistance to it.
RACHEL:	But if it's true, think of the contribution you could make, just by playing baseball.
JACKIE:	In a way, it's a big step toward all kinds of integration, isn't it?
NARRATOR 1:	Just then, the phone rang. It was Frank Simms, a journalist from an important African-American weekly newspaper.
FRANK:	I just heard something strange. Are you meeting with Branch Rickey in New York?
NARRATOR 2:	Jackie didn't know whether to be excited or suspicious about the meeting he was about to have in New York. But he knew one thing for sure—something big was happening.

SCENE 3

NARRATOR 1:	On the morning of August 28, 1945, Jackie Robinson knocked on the door of Branch Rickey's office at Ebbet's Field in Brooklyn.
RICKEY:	Come on in, young man. Sit down. My scouts say you're one of the finest players in the Negro leagues. Do you know why I called you here?
JACKIE:	They told me you were thinking of putting together a Negro league team—the Brown Dodgers or something—and might want me to play shortstop.
RICKEY:	Good, that's what I wanted him to tell you. But it's a lie. I'm thinking of offering you a contract, but I'm not putting together any new team. I want you to play for the Dodgers in the major leagues. What do you think?
NARRATOR 2:	Jackie was speechless. He couldn't believe this might really be happening.

RICKEY:	Do you think you're good enough right now to play for our farm team in Montreal?
JACKIE:	Sure.
RICKEY:	I know you're a good ball player. Do you have the character, the guts, to break the color line?
JACKIE:	I think I do.
RICKEY:	I've had you thoroughly investigated, Robinson. In college, you were a superstar in four sports. You also had a reputation for starting fights.
JACKIE:	I have a habit of standing up for myself. Some people don't like that in a black man.
RICKEY:	That's just what I concluded. If you had been white, people would be calling you an intense competitor. But since you're black, they think you're a hothead. That brings me back to the real issue.
NARRATOR 1:	Mr. Rickey leaned close to Jackie.
RICKEY:	I've been trying to integrate baseball for years, but among baseball men, I'm practically alone. I know I've only got one shot at it. I have to pick the right player, because if the first black player fails, there will never be another chance. I think you might be the right player.
JACKIE:	Thank you, sir.
RICKEY:	I wish I could tell you that all you had to do was be a great baseball player on the field, that your hitting and fielding would show everyone that you belonged in the majors.
JACKIE:	But it is how I play that really counts, isn't it?

RICKEY:	It's what ought to count, but people are going to be watching so much more carefully. There are huge numbers of people who are opposed to integrated baseball. They're all around us, and they'll do anything to see us fail. We can't win this thing by fighting. We can never outnumber or overpower the bigots. You'll have to outclass and outplay them.
JACKIE:	I understand.
RICKEY:	Fans in the stands will yell at you, the most horrible things you've ever heard. Players on other teams will try to hurt you. Pitchers will throw at your head. Runners will spike you coming into your base.
JACKIE:	I can handle them.
RICKEY:	But you must not retaliate. You'll simply have to endure the insults, the cuts and bruises, bad calls from umpires, bad service or no service on the road, hostility from your own teammates.
JACKIE:	Mr. Rickey, are you looking for someone who is afraid to fight back?
RICKEY:	I'm looking for someone with the guts *not* to fight back. Can you do that?
NARRATOR 2:	Jackie thought about the question for a long time.
JACKIE:	Yes. I think I can.
RICKEY:	Good. Now you and I must understand each other on this point. For three years I will support and stand by you as long as you don't fight back or argue with anyone. After that, you're free to do what you want.
JACKIE:	Understood.

RICKEY: It will be the hardest thing you've ever done in your life, much harder than the baseball part. But it's the only way we can win this thing. Now, one more thing: we'll have to keep this a secret for as long as possible so our enemies have less of an opportunity to sabotage our efforts.

SCENE 4

NARRATOR 1: The Montreal Royals announced the signing of Jackie Robinson. The press went wild. Overnight, Jackie Robinson became one of the most talked-about people in America.

NARRATOR 2: Jackie married Rachel, and a few weeks later, they headed to Florida for spring training with the Royals.

NARRATOR 1: Their plane was scheduled to stop in New Orleans for fuel on the way. But as soon as they landed, an airline worker beckoned Jackie down the hall. When Jackie came back, he was mad.

JACKIE: They said we had to wait for the next plane because some military personnel had to use our seats. I don't see any soldiers, do you?

RACHEL: No, but let's just go along with it and hope we can leave on the next plane. I'm starving. Let's find something to eat.

NARRATOR 2: When they got to the airport lunch counter, they found other problems.

COUNTERMAN: Sorry, folks. I can't serve you at this counter.

JACKIE: Where can we get some food around here?

COUNTERMAN: I guess I can give you food to take out if you promise to eat it someplace where no one can see you.

JACKIE: Forget it, man.

NARRATOR 1:	Twelve hours later, Jackie and Rachel finally boarded another plane, but when it stopped again the Robinsons had to give their seats to a white couple. Jackie decided that they might do better on a bus.
NARRATOR 2:	But a few hours after they had boarded a Greyhound, they were interrupted again.
BUS DRIVER:	Listen, you two have got to give me these seats. I've got white people who need them. You've got to move to the back.
JACKIE:	But it's packed back there.
BUS DRIVER:	Would you like me to call the White House and ask the President to change the laws? Go on back there.

SCENE 5

NARRATOR 1:	By the time Jackie and Rachel arrived in Daytona Beach, Jackie was furious. When he found out that they could not stay in the hotel with the rest of the team, he was about ready to quit and go home.
NARRATOR 2:	Two important African-American journalists, Wendell Smith and Billy Rowe, were covering Jackie's first spring training, and they became his best friends there. That first night, they had to convince Jackie to stay.
BILLY:	Jackie, you know racism exists all over America; that's nothing new. That's the reason you're down here.
JACKIE:	I can't take a plane, I can't stay with the team in the hotel. I even heard they might have to move the whole team to a new town because the locals might make trouble.
WENDELL:	Jackie, what you are trying to do is much bigger than what happens in this town, or even in the South. It's about changing our whole society.

NARRATOR 1:	As they argued into the night, Jackie finally started to listen to them, and even agree.
WENDELL:	You have a chance to prove to all those white folks that we deserve to participate fully in our society, that they have no right to exclude us from anything that matters.
BILLY:	They'll have to realize that we deserve everything our society has to offer, and that we are willing to fight for it with dignity. But along the way, we're gonna have to take some abuse.
WENDELL:	You knew it was going to be hard, and it's going to get much harder, but if we don't make it this time, there may not be any next time.
NARRATOR 2:	Armed with new determination, Jackie reported to spring training the next morning. Crowds of reporters were there. They reported it this way:
NEWSPAPER:	The white Montreal players have accepted Jackie Robinson as their teammate. There has been no friction.
NARRATOR 1:	Of course the reality was a little different. That first morning a crowd tried to block Jackie's entry onto the field. He had to find a hole in the back of the fence and crawl through it.
NARRATOR 2:	Tension was high on and off the field at the Royals camp. Team manager, Clay Hopper, had begged Rickey not to sign Jackie.
NARRATOR 1:	Once, Mr. Rickey and Clay Hopper were watching practice, when Jackie made an amazing play in the field.
RICKEY:	Did you see that, Hopper? That play was superhuman!
HOPPER:	Mr. Rickey, do you really think so? After all, he's only a black player.
NARRATOR 2:	Rickey, stunned, didn't answer. He knew that racism had been bred so deeply into Clay Hopper that no conversation was going to change things. It would take some time.

SCENE 6

NARRATOR 1: Clay Hopper and most of the players barely tolerated Jackie's presence. But there was more serious resistance from the community.

NARRATOR 2: Like the time the Royals played the Jersey Giants in Sanford, Florida. They had just arrived when Branch Rickey walked up to Jackie.

RICKEY: Jack, the local sheriff says he's going to close us down if you play today. They have a law against integrated baseball and he's going to enforce it.

JACKIE: I don't care, I'm going to play. He's going to have to come out and get me.

RICKEY: That's what I was hoping you'd say.

NARRATOR 1: In the first inning, Jackie came up to bat and hit a clean single. He stole second and came sliding home on another hit. But when he got back on his feet, he saw the sheriff standing over him.

SHERIFF: This game is officially over. Here in Sanford, we've never allowed blacks on the field with whites, and we ain't gonna start today.

NARRATOR 2: Jackie went back and sat on the bench, but the sheriff was still following him.

SHERIFF: We don't allow blacks on the white bench, either.

NARRATOR 1: During every game, fans yelled insults and threats.

NARRATOR 2: Most of Jackie's teammates were unfriendly.

NARRATOR 1: As a player, Jackie looked pretty ordinary out there. It was hard for him to concentrate on baseball. People wondered if he was good enough to play in the minor leagues.

NARRATOR 2: All that wondering stopped during the Royals' first regular season game, against the Jersey Giants.

NARRATOR 1: That day, Jackie Robinson got four hits, including a home run, and led his team to a 14–0 rout of the Jersey Giants. But what really excited the crowd was his base running.

ANNOUNCER: Robinson lays down a beautiful bunt and he's on first base . . . And now, with the count two and one, Robinson takes off for second. Look at him go. He's in with a stolen base.

NARRATOR 2: The next batter singled Jackie over to third base.

ANNOUNCER: Now, Robinson is dancing off third. The pitcher throws to third but not in time. Now Robinson breaks for home, but he's only bluffing.

NARRATOR 1: Within a few minutes, Jackie made the pitcher so nervous that he lost his concentration and balked the run in.

ANNOUNCER: Robinson trots home. I'll tell you, I've never seen anything like this before. Jackie Robinson just created that run all by himself.

NARRATOR 2: Jackie's year in the minor leagues was filled with ups and downs. When the Royals played in many American cities, Jackie was met with taunts, hate mail and real threats of violence. On other days, he faced supportive crowds who just wanted to see good baseball, and didn't care about his color.

NARRATOR 1: In Montreal, where the Royals played their home games, race was no issue at all. Jackie was the fan's favorite.

NARRATOR 2: When he led the Royals to a championship in the minor league World Series, the fans carried him off the field on their shoulders. Clay Hopper, the manager who had begged Rickey not to sign Jackie, offered him his hand.

HOPPER: You're a great ball player and a fine gentleman. It's been a pleasure having you on the team.

NARRATOR 1: Although he didn't know it yet, Jackie's next stop was the major leagues.

SCENE 8

NEWSPAPER: APRIL 9, 1947: The Brooklyn Dodgers today purchased the contract of Jack Roosevelt Robinson, infielder . . .

NARRATOR 2: Jackie Robinson's first week as a Brooklyn Dodger was ordinary. He did well in the field and got a few hits. The first bad racial incident came the first time he played in Philadelphia.

NARRATOR 1: The Phillies' manager, Ben Chapman, was a known racist who had been in trouble as a player for yelling anti-Semitic slurs at fans.

NARRATOR 2: Chapman got his Phillies players to join him in unleashing a series-long flood of racial epithets at Jackie.

NARRATOR 1: At first, Jackie could barely stand to take all the abuse without answering back. But he remembered the deal he had made. He had to keep his cool. Soon his teammates began to sense the unfairness of Jackie's situation.

NARRATOR 2: Finally, in the third game, one Dodger teammate, Eddie Stanky, came out of the dugout and yelled at the Phillies.

EDDIE: Hey, you cowards! Why don't you pick on someone who can answer back!

NARRATOR 1: It was a small gesture, but that and other events began to unify the Dodgers around Jackie. They began to realize that he was not only a great baseball player but a tremendous person, and there was no legitimate reason to exclude him.

EPILOGUE

NARRATOR 2: Jackie Robinson continued to play quietly through the trials of racism and hatred. On the field he excelled, winning Rookie of the Year honors in 1947, and later winning batting titles and even the American League Most Valuable Player award. The grace, restraint, and intelligence he displayed on and off the field made it impossible for even the worst racists to argue for keeping African Americans out of baseball.

NARRATOR 1: Although many players who followed Jackie into the major leagues also faced racism, Jackie had blazed a trail. His entry into baseball is regarded by many people as the first event of the modern civil rights movement. After he retired from baseball, Robinson fought for civil rights as a columnist and public speaker. Martin Luther King, Jr., said: "Jackie Robinson made it possible for me in the first place. Without him I could never have done what I did." Jackie Robinson died in 1972, at the age of fifty-three.

Jackie Robinson

Background

Jack Roosevelt Robinson was born on January 31, 1919, to parents who share-cropped on a Georgia plantation. When Jackie was young, his father left home, and soon after, his mother moved the family to California. Jackie attended Pasadena Junior College before moving on to UCLA. There he was a star in baseball, football, track, and basketball. Some people labeled him "the finest athlete in America." While in school, Jackie met Rachel Isum, whom he later married. He left UCLA before graduating, in order to support his mother, then entered the army, where he was a lieutenant during World War II.

After being discharged, Robinson joined the Kansas City Monarchs, then a team in the Negro American League. In 1947, he was asked to play for the Brooklyn Dodgers, thus becoming the first African American to play major league baseball. During his career with the Dodgers, Jackie won Rookie of the Year and Most Valuable Player awards and led the team to a World Series title in 1955. He retired in 1957.

In 1962, in his first year of eligibility, he was the first African American inducted into the Baseball Hall of Fame. After retiring from baseball, he was instrumental in working for political change as a member of the National Association for the Advancement of Colored People (NAACP). Jackie Robinson was 53 when he died in 1972.

For Discussion

DECISIONS, DECISIONS

In making major decisions, we often compose a list of pros and cons. Ask students what they think might have been on Jackie Robinson's list when he was offered the position on the Brooklyn Dodgers. What might have been on Branch Rickey's list when he thought about hiring African-American players for the Dodgers? As students respond, add to a pros and cons list on the chalkboard or overhead.

FIGHTING BACK

Jackie Robinson did not fight back in the traditional way when other players and the fans demonstrated their prejudice. Ask students to consider what might have happened if he had. How did he fight back in his own way? Continue the discussion by asking students what strategies they might use to fight back that don't involve violence.

WHAT MAKES A HERO?

Jackie Robinson is a hero to many people. Ask students if there are any of them who might choose Jackie Robinson as a hero. Have them brainstorm the characteristics and/or actions that made him a hero. Invite students to share who else are their heroes. Encourage them to explain why and ask them to consider how their choice might have been different if Jackie Robinson hadn't broken the color barrier in baseball.

Write About It

IN MY OPINION

After the Dodgers played the Phillies, many national newspapers were filled with stories of the Phillies' bad behavior. Editorials lambasted the Phillies, their manager, and their fans. Ask students to write a news story or an editorial about the incident.

THE NEGRO BASEBALL LEAGUE

Before Jackie Robinson broke the color barrier in baseball, African-American players had formed their own baseball leagues—the Negro leagues. Encourage students to find out more about the players, teams, or history of these leagues. They can then present their research in the form of an article for a sports magazine.

TRADING CARDS

From his days with the Kansas City Monarchs to his retirement from the Brooklyn Dodgers, Jackie Robinson's career was highlighted by honors. Invite students to design baseball cards for different years in Robinson's career. They should include a photo or illustration of Robinson on the front of the cards and biographical and statistical information on the back.

Additional Reading

Black Diamond: The Story of the Negro Baseball Leagues by Patricia C. and Frederick McKissack, Jr. (Scholastic, 1998)

In the Year of the Boar and Jackie Robinson by Bette Bao Lord (HarperCollins, 1986)

Jackie Robinson Breaks the Color Line by Andrew Santella (Scholastic, 1996)

Jackie's Nine: Jackie Robinson's Values to Live By by Sharon Robinson (Scholastic, 2000)

QUOTES

I guess if I could choose one of the most important moments in my life, I would go back to 1947, in the Yankee Stadium in New York City. It was the opening day of the World Series and I was for the first time playing in the series as a member of the Brooklyn Dodgers team.

I want to be free to follow the dictates of my own mind and conscience without being subject to the pressures of any man, black or white. I think that is what most people of all races want.

A life is not important, except in the impact is has on other lives.

Thurgood Marshall
The Fight for Equal Justice

by Jacqueline Charlesworth

EQUAL JUSTICE UNDER LAW

>> Characters <<

Narrators 1 and 2

William Marshall, Sr.,
Thurgood's father

Thurgood Marshall

William Marshall, Jr.,
Thurgood's brother

Norma Marshall,
Thurgood's mother

NAACP Staff
Attorneys 1 and 2

Police Officers 1–4

Justices of the Supreme
Court 1–7
(nonspeaking roles)

Felix Frankfurter,
*Justice of the
Supreme Court*

Earl Warren,
*Chief Justice of the
Supreme Court*

Reporters 1 and 2

Lyndon B. Johnson,
*President of the
United States*

INTRODUCTION

NARRATOR 1: After the Civil War, black children started going to school, but, especially in the South, they often had to attend different schools from the white children—a practice called segregation. These schools often had fewer teachers and supplies than the white schools. On May 17, 1954, the Supreme Court of the United States issued an opinion that said segregation in the school was illegal, and black children must be allowed to go to school with white children.

NARRATOR 2: Many consider the opinion, called *Brown v. Board of Education*, to be the most important decision the Supreme Court has ever made. The justices on the Court had taken a stand. They said the Constitution stood for real equality—even though they knew that many white people would be angry and would fight hard to keep black children out of "their" schools. A black man was responsible for persuading the justices to do the right thing. That man was a lawyer named Thurgood Marshall.

SCENE 1

NARRATOR 1: In the kitchen of a middle-class black home in Baltimore, Maryland, in 1918, Norma Marshall is at the stove. Her husband William is at the kitchen table with their son, also named William.

NARRATOR 2: Thurgood Marshall was named after his grandfather on his father's side, a former slave. His grandfather had chosen to call himself Thoroughgood when he joined the Union Army to fight against slavery during the Civil War. When the younger Thoroughgood was in second grade, he decided that his name was too long and shortened it to Thurgood.

NARRATOR 1:	Thurgood's mother, Norma Arica, was a schoolteacher at an all-black elementary school. His father, William, worked for the Baltimore & Ohio railroad as a dining-car waiter, which was considered a good job for an African-American man in those days. And there was one other member of the family, Thurgood's older brother, also named William.
NARRATOR 2:	Ten-year-old Thurgood trudges in and throws his schoolbooks onto the table.
WILLIAM, SR.:	Why, son, what's got into you? And why are you so late in coming home?
THURGOOD:	I had to stay after school again.
WILLIAM, JR.:	Let me guess—your big mouth got you into trouble again!
NORMA:	William, right now you're the one with the big mouth. All right, Thurgood, what happened this time?
WILLIAM, SR.:	Norma, you know Thurgood's just a high-spirited boy. Takes after his great-grandfather, brought all the way over here from Africa. The way folks tell it, that man was so feisty, his owner had no choice but to set him free! Now, son, go on and tell us what happened.
THURGOOD:	During geography, Fred leaned over and asked if I thought the kids in white school were as bored as we were. I was just going to tell him that I didn't understand why there should be separate schools for whites, but in any case I doubted geography could ever be interesting—when the teacher told us we'd have to stay after school because we were talking. She said we couldn't leave until after we had memorized another piece of the Constitution.
NORMA:	Which piece was it this time?

THURGOOD:	*(reciting from the Fourteenth Amendment)* No state shall make or enforce any law which shall abridge the privileges or immunities of citizens of the United States; nor shall any state deprive any person of life, liberty, or property, without due process of law; nor deny to any person within its jurisdiction the equal protection of the laws.
WILLIAM, SR.:	Do you know what that means?
THURGOOD:	It seems like a long way of saying that all citizens of the United States are supposed to be treated the same under the law.
NORMA:	Good for you, Thurgood! Seeing as how you take after your great-grandfather, I think you're going to know the whole Constitution before you get out of grade school. How about some supper?

SCENE 2

NARRATOR 1:	After graduating from college, Thurgood knew he wanted to be a lawyer. When he was turned down by the all-white University of Maryland, he enrolled in the law school of Howard University, a prestigious black institution, where he quickly became a top student.
NARRATOR 2:	One of Thurgood's professors at Howard was so impressed with his student that he later offered Thurgood a job with the National Association for the Advancement of Colored People, or NAACP, a group dedicated to helping African Americans achieve equality. As an NAACP lawyer, Thurgood traveled around the country fighting for the rights of African Americans in courts. Sometimes, the job was dangerous.
NARRATOR 1:	On a dark night in Columbia, Tennessee, in 1946, Thurgood and two other NAACP lawyers are driving back to their hotel in Nashville after a long day in court.
THURGOOD:	*(at the wheel)* Whew! I would say that was a good day's work!

STAFF ATTORNEY 1: Yeah, twenty-four of our brothers out of jail—one to go!

STAFF ATTORNEY 2: I can't imagine what those white cops were thinking—arresting twenty-five men for attempted murder. It's the cops who raided a black neighborhood, not vice versa! There's not a shred of evidence against any of those defendants.

THURGOOD: *(looking into rear-view mirror with sounds of sirens approaching)* Speaking of cops, we're about to get pulled over.

NARRATOR 2: As the siren grows louder, Thurgood pulls the car over to the side of the road. Three police cars pull up behind, and in a moment, the lawyers' car is surrounded by four white police officers.

OFFICER 1: Everyone out of the car! Now!

THURGOOD: *(The three lawyers get out of the car.)* Excuse me officer, but can you tell me what the problem is?

OFFICER 2: We'll let you know when we find it. Now get out!

OFFICER 1: These black lawyers think they're so smart, but I wouldn't be surprised to find out they're carrying some illegal liquor with them. Search the car, men! *(Officers 3 and 4 search car but find nothing.)*

OFFICER 3: I don't see anything, boss. Just a bunch of law books and papers.

OFFICER 4: Don't you worry. We'll get 'em next time!

OFFICER 2: All right, boys, you can go on—this time—but you better hightail it out of town.

NARRATOR 1: Thurgood felt lucky that he made it back to Nashville that night. Even though the incident had shaken him up, he returned to the town of Columbia the next week to obtain the release of the last of the twenty-five accused African-American men.

SCENE 3

NARRATOR 2: Inside the Supreme Court in Washington, D.C., on December 9, 1952, nine white men in black robes sit in a row behind a high table at one end of the room. The overflow audience includes many lawyers and reporters who have come to listen to the case called *Brown v. Board of Education* being argued.

THURGOOD: Your honors, the Fourteenth Amendment of the Constitution is a guarantee of equality to black and white children alike. There is no evidence that black children do not have the same ability to learn as white children. What the evidence does show is that forcing black children to attend separate schools hurts them because it teaches them they are not as good as white children.

JUSTICE FRANKFURTER: Mr. Marshall, don't you think we just have to recognize certain facts of life? That this is the way some people want to live?

THURGOOD: Your honor, to accept segregation as a fact of life is to accept that black children don't deserve full equality. The Court should make clear that that is not what our Constitution stands for.

SCENE 4

NARRATOR 1: Inside the Supreme Court, about a year and a half later...

JUSTICE WARREN: *(clearing throat)* I have for announcement the judgment and opinion of the Court in *Brown v. Board of Education*, in which young black students have challenged the constitutionality of public schools that segregate students by race.

REPORTER 1: *(whispering to Reporter 2, who's dozing off)* Hey, wake up! It's the *Brown* decision.

REPORTER 2: *(almost jumping up)* It's about time!

JUSTICE WARREN: *(continuing)* To answer the question presented by this case, we must look at the effect of segregation on public education. Today, education is perhaps the most important function of the state and local governments. It is doubtful that any child may reasonably be expected to succeed in life if he is denied the opportunity of an education. Such an opportunity must be provided on equal terms. Does segregation of children in public school solely on the basis of race deprive the children of the minority group of educational opportunities? *(slight pause)* We believe that it does.

REPORTER 2: *(whispering to Reporter 1 as they write quickly in their notebooks)* Wow! This is really big! The Court just struck down segregation in the schools!

JUSTICE WARREN: *(continuing)* To separate some children from others of similar age and qualifications solely because of their race generates a feeling of inferiority as to their status in the community, which may affect their hearts and minds in a way unlikely ever to be undone. And so, today we declare segregation to be unconstitutional.

SCENE 5

NARRATOR 2: After winning the *Brown* case, Thurgood continued his legal battles on behalf of African Americans. In 1961, recognizing how much Thurgood had helped shape the law in the area of civil rights, President John F. Kennedy nominated him to be a judge on the federal appeals court in New York. A few years later, President Lyndon B. Johnson chose Thurgood to be Solicitor General, a high-ranking legal position in the United States government. There was more in store for the famous civil rights lawyer.

NARRATOR 1: In the White House Rose Garden, June 13, 1967, a crowd of reporters with television cameras and microphones waits for President Johnson to begin a news conference.

REPORTER 2: What do you suppose this is all about? My boss told me to get here on the double.

REPORTER 1: It's got to be the Supreme Court vacancy. Wait a minute—here comes the President. Look! He's got Thurgood Marshall with him.

REPORTER 2: The Solicitor General?

PRESIDENT JOHNSON: (*standing at the podium*) I have gathered you here today to announce that I am nominating Thurgood Marshall to become a Justice of the Supreme Court of the United States of America. He has served this nation well as Solicitor General, and I believe he will continue to do so on the Supreme Court.

REPORTERS 1 AND 2: (*waving hands in air*) Mr. President! Over here! Mr. President!

PRESIDENT JOHNSON: (*pointing to Reporter 1*) You, there.

REPORTER 1: Mr. President, there has never before been a black man on the Supreme Court. Is that why you chose Thurgood Marshall?

PRESIDENT JOHNSON: I chose him because he deserves the appointment. Thurgood Marshall is the best qualified by training and by very valuable service to the country. (*pause*) I believe it is the right thing to do, the right time to do it, the right man, and the right place. (*turning to Thurgood*) Now . . . would you like to say a few words?

THURGOOD: (*stepping up to the podium*) Mr. President, it is with great pride that I accept the honor you bestow upon me today. I will do my best to live up to it. On the front of the Supreme Court building it says "Equal Justice Under Law." I have entered that building many times and never stopped believing in those words, because in my lifetime I have seen that law can change things for the better— even the hearts of men.

Thurgood Marshall

Background

Thurgood Marshall was born on July 2, 1908, in West Baltimore, Maryland. After graduating with honors from Lincoln University, the nation's oldest black college, Thurgood went to law school at Howard University. While at Howard, he married Vivian Burey.

In 1936, Charles Houston asked Thurgood to join him as an NAACP staff attorney; Thurgood took over as head lawyer in 1938. During his years as a civil rights advocate, Thurgood won the majority of the cases he argued before the Supreme Court, including *Brown v. Board of Education*, the landmark 1954 decision outlawing racial segregation in public schools. Soon after the *Brown* victory, Thurgood's wife died of cancer. He married his second wife, Cecilia Suyat, an NAACP secretary, at the end of 1955.

In 1961, President John F. Kennedy appointed Thurgood to be a judge on the United States Court of Appeals of the Second Circuit. Thurgood served on that court until 1965, when President Lyndon B. Johnson chose him to be Solicitor General. In 1967, President Johnson nominated Thurgood to be a justice of the United States Supreme Court. He retired in 1991, but left his mark as an ardent defender of the rights of minorities and women. When asked by a reporter why he was stepping down, Marshall said he was "getting old and coming apart." Thurgood Marshall died of heart failure in Bethesda, Maryland, on January 24, 1993.

For Discussion

EQUALITY FOR ALL

Review the examples of racism in the play— for example, segregated schools or the behavior of the white police. Talk about instances of racism or discrimination that your students have experienced or witnessed. What kinds of remedies can they think of to apply to those situations?

A POSITIVE PUNISHMENT

When Thurgood Marshall misbehaved in grade school, the principal would make him memorize a part of the Constitution. Emphasizing the positive impact that had on Thurgood's life, have kids memorize (or read) a line or two of the Constitution. After they recite the lines to the class, they can then explain the meaning in their own words.

INTEGRATION TODAY

Encourage students to think about ways that integration could be improved in schools today. Tell them that integration can mean not only the actual makeup of the student body but also how well students mix within the school—in classes, social situations, sports teams, and so on. As a class, brainstorm at least three positive suggestions for encouraging greater integration.

Write About It

A BRIEF APPEARANCE

Before lawyers argue cases before the Supreme Court, they give the justices written versions of their arguments, called briefs, so the justices are familiar with the points of their arguments. Ask students to help Thurgood Marshall prepare his brief against segregation. They should include at least three arguments against segregation. Remind students that since the best briefs are logical and well-organized, they might want to use a five-paragraph format: an introduction, one paragraph discussing each reason, and a summary.

A LONG TIME IN COMING

Thurgood Marshall helped change the role of African Americans in our society. Have students create time lines depicting landmarks in the struggle for black equality. They may wish to start with the emancipation Proclamation in 1863 and continue to the present day. After students compare and discuss their time lines, ask them to compile their information into one class time line.

ACTS OF BRAVERY

As a result of *Brown v. Board of Education*, public schools began to integrate slowly. Have students research the experiences of some of the brave students, such as Ruby Bridges and the Little Rock Nine, who were some of the first to venture into integrated schools.

Additional Reading

Remember: The Journey to School Integration by Toni Morrison (Houghton Mifflin, 2004)

Thurgood Marshall: Champion of Justice by G.S. Prentzas (Chelsea House, 1993)

Thurgood Marshall and the Supreme Court by Deborah Kent (Scholastic, 1997)

QUOTES

I don't know of any president who ever came out, four-square, for ending all segregation in all places. I think it would be good for a president to say, "People are people. Take the skin off, there's no difference." I think it would be good to say so.

....

I think the Constitution is the greatest body of laws ever, and what to me and to many people is so extraordinary about it is that in this late day you find that it works. I don't know of any better job that could have been done . . . . If you read it with any understanding, there's hardly anything that it doesn't cover.

The Rosa Parks Story

by Jonathan Blum

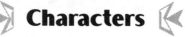
Characters

Narrators 1 and 2

Leona McCauley,
Rosa's mother

Rosa McCauley,
later Rosa Parks

Johnnie, *Rosa's
childhood girlfriend*

Rowena,
a classmate of Rosa's

Miss Barton,
Rosa's teacher

Raymond Parks,
a barber

Barbershop patron

Bus driver

E. D. Nixon,
*President of NAACP,
Montgomery Chapter*

Clerk

Officer

Dr. Martin Luther
King, Jr.

Lawyer, *Rosa's lawyer*

Judge

SCENE 1

NARRATOR 1:   It is 1924, in Montgomery, Alabama. Leona McCauley is taking her eleven-year-old daughter, Rosa, to a new school.

LEONA: Remember, this school costs money.

ROSA: Yes, ma'am.

LEONA: Speak only when you're spoken to. But if the teacher asks a question and you know the answer, open your mouth. Don't be shy. Let her know you're a smart girl.

NARRATOR 2:   During lunch in the schoolyard, Rosa makes a friend.

JOHNNIE: Are you from the country?

ROSA: Yes, an area called Pine Level.

JOHNNIE: I've heard of that, but I don't know where it is. My name is Rebecca Daniels, but you can call me Johnnie. What do you think of the new school so far?

ROSA: It's different from what I'm used to.

JOHNNIE: Bet this is the first schoolroom you were in with desks to write on and glass in the windows. You've never seen a chalkboard before, or had a white teacher, right?

ROSA: How do you know all this?

JOHNNIE: Only country girls eat tomato sandwiches.

NARRATOR 1:   In class, the teacher, Miss Barton, tells one girl, Rowena, she did not do well on a test.

ROWENA: Why do we even bother with reading and arithmetic when all we're going to end up doing for jobs is washing somebody's clothes and wiping their babies' snotty noses?

MISS BARTON:	Who wants to answer Rowena's question? Rosa, why do we bother?
ROSA:	We bother so that we can be equal to everybody else.
ROWENA:	We're not equal to everybody else. We're not equal to white folks.
ROSA:	I was raised to believe that if I put my mind to it, I could do whatever I wanted in the world. I was taught that no one is better than I am. No man, no woman, black or white.
ROWENA:	But if white folks say . . .
ROSA:	No one. A person can take everything from you, even your life. But they can't take away your dignity. Nobody can take that from you but you. My grandfather told me that and—I believe it.
MISS BARTON:	I hope that everyone in this class remembers what Rosa just taught you.

SCENE 2

NARRATOR 2:	It is 1931, on a rainy afternoon in Montgomery. Raymond Parks, a barber, and his patron discuss the sentencing of the Scottsboro boys. The Scottsboro boys were nine black youths convicted of assaulting two young white women in northern Alabama.
RAYMOND:	We're working against time to free those boys.
BARBERSHOP PATRON:	At least most of them are off death row.
RAYMOND:	But they're still facing seventy-five to ninety-nine years in prison. They need better lawyers. That's why I'm working with a group here in Montgomery to raise money.
BARBER SHOP PATRON:	It's dangerous business, Parks.

RAYMOND:	It may be, but life is about facing danger and taking risks. We have to stand up for what's right, even if it means putting our lives on the line.
NARRATOR 1:	Rosa, now in high school, walks past the barbershop. Raymond steps outside and hands her a copy of a local African-American newspaper.
RAYMOND:	I'm working on the Scottsboro boys' legal defense fund. I think every black person in this town should be supporting those boys.
NARRATOR 2:	Rosa looks down at the newspaper and begins to read. It contains dangerous language that makes Rosa wary.
ROSA:	Thanks for the paper, but I'd better be getting home.

SCENE 3

NARRATOR 1:	Later that week, Rosa and her mother discuss the case, which now has the attention of the National Association for the Advancement of Colored People, or NAACP.
ROSA:	Those boys didn't assault those white girls, and everybody knows it. The NAACP is coming down from New York to take up their case.
LEONA:	They're just going to make it worse for everybody.
ROSA:	Mama, several of the boys have been sentenced to die. How much worse can it get?
NARRATOR 2:	At the front door, Raymond arrives. Rosa tells her mom to tell him she's not home. He leaves and comes back another day, but Rosa still will not see him. On his third visit, Rosa finally agrees to go out with him. They go down to the river's edge.
ROSA:	Do you like to fish? My grandfather taught me how.

NARRATOR 1: Raymond and Rosa talk and fish. Rosa tells Raymond about her grandfather, whom she loved dearly. Raymond tells Rosa about his father—a mean, light-skinned man who tried to pass for white. Raymond and Rosa's friendship grows.

SCENE 4

NARRATOR 2: The following week, Rosa finds out that Raymond has gone to support the protests in Scottsboro. She knows he will face racial hatred, and she fears for his life.

NARRATOR 1: When Raymond finally returns and visits her, she hugs him with tears in her eyes.

ROSA: I thought you were dead.

RAYMOND: I'm fine. As long as I have you, I don't need anything else.

NARRATOR 2: In 1932, Rosa and Raymond Parks marry.

SCENE 5

NARRATOR 1: Ten years later, Rosa is working as a seamstress at the Montgomery Fair department store. She rides the bus to and from work.

NARRATOR 2: The buses in Montgomery are segregated. Black riders must pay their fare, step off the bus, and enter at the back.

NARRATOR 1: One evening, Rosa pays her fare, then walks to her seat from the front of the bus.

BUS DRIVER: To ride this bus, you have to step off and enter in the back.

ROSA: I'm already on. Besides, it's raining.

NARRATOR 2: The bus driver approaches Rosa.

BUS DRIVER: I don't care if the sky is falling. If you're going to ride my bus, you get off and enter round the back. Do you hear me?

ROSA:	*(angrily)* Do not put your hands on me.
NARRATOR 1:	Rosa gets off and walks home five miles in the rain. When she gets home, her mother notices her wet clothes.
LEONA:	What happened? Did you miss the bus?
ROSA:	I was kicked off.
LEONA:	Why?
ROSA:	Because I did not want to get off and enter in the back. The dime I pay to ride is the same color as the dime white folks use! We are paying to be humiliated.

SCENE 6

NARRATOR 2:	Rosa learns that her old friend Johnnie now works for the Montgomery office of the NAACP. One day Rosa visits Johnnie. While there, she meets the NAACP Montgomery president E. D. Nixon and volunteers to be a secretary in the office.
NIXON:	We also need someone to oversee the Youth Council, advise school-age kids, lead Bible study, and teach self-esteem.
ROSA:	I'd love to!
JOHNNIE:	She'll be perfect.
NARRATOR 1:	When Raymond hears that Rosa has taken a leadership role at the NAACP, he is concerned for her safety. Still, he supports her.
NARRATOR 2:	A few days later at a nearby park, Rosa and Johnnie reminisce about their school days.
JOHNNIE:	Remember when you first came to Montgomery? You didn't know yet that colored folk couldn't try things on at the stores. You had never had a new pair of shoes.
ROSA:	When you went to buy some, I asked you, "Why is the salesman tracing a copy of your feet?"

JOHNNIE:	You had never seen separate water fountains before.
ROSA:	I used to wonder if water in the white fountains tasted better. It didn't.
JOHNNIE:	That was such a long time ago. Some things have changed, but much still needs to be done. Rosa, are you registered to vote?
ROSA:	Not yet.
JOHNNIE:	If Mr. Nixon finds out, he'll lecture you: "Black folks who don't vote deserve the treatment they get."
ROSA:	Then I'll register right away.

SCENE 7

NARRATOR 1:	Before Rosa can register to vote, she has to take a civics test.
CLERK:	You didn't pass.
ROSA:	I would like the test back, please.
CLERK:	That's against policy.
ROSA:	Well, how will I know which questions I got wrong?
NARRATOR 2:	The clerk refuses to give Rosa her test back. She goes home and discusses her anger with Raymond.
ROSA:	Whites can register to vote with ease. As a U.S. citizen, I have a right to vote. No person can keep me from that right.
NARRATOR 1:	Rosa returns to the registration office and takes the test again.
ROSA:	If you say I didn't pass this time, I'll bring a lawyer to find out which answers I got wrong.
NARRATOR 2:	But Rosa passes the test, and the clerk registers her to vote.

SCENE 8

NARRATOR 1: It is now 1955. Many leaders are struggling to find solutions to make Montgomery bus drivers treat African-American riders as equal human beings.

NARRATOR 2: During the holiday season, Rosa's boss offers her extra hours sewing at the department store.

NARRATOR 1: On Thursday, December 1, after work, Rosa boards a city bus. She sits with three other black passengers in the fifth row of the black section. A few stops later, the first four rows fill with whites; one white man is left standing. By law, whites and blacks may not sit in the same row.

BUS DRIVER: Let me have those front seats.

NARRATOR 2: The three others in Rosa's row get up. Rosa remains seated.

BUS DRIVER: Are you going to move?

NARRATOR 1: Rosa cannot take this treatment any longer. She looks at the driver and makes a historic decision.

ROSA: (softly) No.

BUS DRIVER: Give me that seat or I'm going to have you arrested.

ROSA: (softly) You may do that.

NARRATOR 2: The driver calls the police.

OFFICER: Why won't you stand up?

ROSA: Why do you all push us around?

OFFICER: The law is the law, lady. You're under arrest.

SCENE 9

NARRATOR 1:	When Nixon phones the police to find out what happened, the officers will not give him any information about Rosa's arrest.
NARRATOR 2:	Nixon and Raymond, along with a lawyer, post bond and get Rosa out of jail. Raymond hugs Rosa.
RAYMOND:	Everything will be all right. Your case is going to court on Monday. Did you put her up to this, Nixon?
NIXON:	If anything, she's the one leading us.
ROSA:	I did not ask to be arrested, Raymond. I wanted exactly what everybody else on that bus wanted—to go home. I don't need the NAACP or anybody else to tell me that I have a right to my own dignity.
NARRATOR 1:	That night, leaders begin organizing the city's African Americans to boycott the buses on Monday.
NARRATOR 2:	A meeting to finalize details of a boycott is held at the Dexter Avenue Baptist Church, where a new minister, the Reverend Dr. Martin Luther King, Jr., presides. Many disagreements take place at the meeting.
DR. KING:	If the protest against the buses is going to work, it's critical that we be together. Divisiveness is the sure path to failure.

SCENE 10

NARRATOR 1:	When Monday arrives, Rosa's lawyer argues her case in court.
LAWYER:	My client was within her lawful rights not to give up her seat on the bus.
JUDGE:	The court has heard both sides and finds Mrs. Rosa Parks guilty of disorderly conduct. The fine is ten dollars.

NARRATOR 2:	Meanwhile, bus after empty bus rolls down the streets of Montgomery. The boycott is a huge success.
NARRATOR 1:	That night, a large gathering of black citizens agrees to continue the boycott.
DR. KING:	We are determined here in Montgomery to work and fight until justice runs down like water and righteousness like a mighty stream!
NARRATOR 2:	A private taxi plan is set up where blacks with cars offer rides to those without. Many white businesses lose money. Rosa loses her job.

SCENE 11

NARRATOR 1:	At home, stalkers threaten Rosa and her husband. Rosa also worries that she is losing Raymond. Her mother comforts her.
ROSA:	We had to board up the house for safety today. Raymond told me he can't take much more of this.
LEONA:	That day on the bus, you were just being who you are. Raymond loves you for it, and I love you, too.
NARRATOR 2:	The bus boycott continues into 1956. Dr. King's and E. D. Nixon's homes are bombed. But black citizens do not give up their cause. The civil rights movement is underway.
NARRATOR 1:	Rosa works out of the house as a private seamstress. One night, she and Raymond find a peaceful moment.
RAYMOND:	Rosa, you've made a lot of people change the way they think about themselves and how they treat others.
ROSA:	Raymond, I never meant for what I did to change things between us.
RAYMOND:	Well, it did. But it was a good change—although it took me a while to see it.

NARRATOR 2:   On November 13, 1956, while the Montgomery bus boycott was still going strong, the U.S. Supreme Court declared segregation on buses unconstitutional.

NARRATOR 1:   Rosa Parks changed the world by refusing to give up her seat to a white man. Her brave action was a key triumph of the civil rights movement.

Rosa Parks

Background

Rosa Parks was born on February 4, 1913, in Tuskegee, Alabama. Her father was a carpenter; her mother was a teacher. In 1932, Rosa married Raymond Parks. Like her husband, she was a member of the NAACP and fought for the right to become a registered voter.

One night in December 1955, Rosa Parks was riding a bus home from work when she refused to give up her seat to a white man. She was arrested and jailed for two-and-a-half hours, then convicted of breaking the segregation law and fined $14. She lost her job as a seamstress in a department store. The people of Montgomery rallied behind her by boycotting the bus company. Led by Martin Luther King, Jr., the protest continued for more than a year, until the U.S. Supreme Court declared that Alabama's bus segregation laws were unconstitutional.

After the boycott, Rosa and her family moved to Detroit, Michigan, where her husband died in 1977. In 1987, she started the Raymond and Rosa Parks Institute for Self-Development, an organization to teach young people how to help themselves and their communities. Rosa Parks was also elected to the board of the NAACP. Because of her courage and determination, Rosa Parks is known as the "Mother of the Civil Rights Movement."

For Discussion

MAKING A DIFFERENCE

Rosa Parks's refusal to give up her seat on a city bus set off a chain reaction of events— from a bus boycott to a landmark decision by the Supreme Court. One woman's actions reverberated throughout her community and eventually the entire country. Discuss with students whether or not they feel one person can make a difference in fighting injustice. Ask them to share their opinions about other role models who they think have made a difference in their community, the country, or the world.

BOYCOTT: PROS AND CONS

The word *boycott* comes from the name of Irish landowner Charles C. Boycott, who was ostracized for not lowering rents on his property in 1897. Discuss the bus boycott in Montgomery and its results. Do students think a boycott is an effective form of protest? Ask them to consider what would happen if people stopped shopping at a local store. What would happen to the people who own the store? How would the boycott affect the workers and their families? In what ways would the rest of the community be affected? What kinds of sacrifices would people on both sides of the boycott have to make?

DISCRIMINATION DAY

Rosa Parks and the African-American citizens of Montgomery experienced discrimination firsthand. Have your students ever been discriminated against because of who they are? If so, was it age, race, gender, or something else that sparked the discrimination? What did they do, or wish they had done, to protest the discrimination? Would a boycott against the offending party have been practical?

Write About It

DEAR ROSA PARKS

Rosa Parks is considered to be the "Mother of the Civil Rights Movement." Let students compose letters to Mrs. Parks. They may wish to applaud her courage, ask her questions about her life, or find out more about the Rosa and Raymond Parks Institute for Self-Development.

CIVIL RIGHTS HALL OF FAME

Rosa Parks and many other people were active in the civil rights movement. Set aside space in the classroom so that students can construct their own Civil Rights Hall of Fame. Each student can nominate someone for the Hall of Fame by preparing a report highlighting that person's role in the civil rights movement. Any photos, illustrations, or other relevant artifacts will help round out the exhibit.

SPREAD THE NEWS

The Women's Political Caucus handed out leaflets to spread news about the Montgomery bus boycott. Before students begin the following activity, discuss leaflets with them. Do they recall any leaflets they have seen? If so, why do those in particular stick in their minds? Mention that since the amount of space on a leaflet is limited, the message has to be short; only the most pertinent information is included, and illustrations and graphics are used to highlight certain things. Have students write and design their own leaflets telling about Rosa Parks, the boycott, the reason for it, and the meeting at the church.

Additional Reading

Montgomery Bus Boycott by R. Conrad Stein (Scholastic, 1993)

Rosa Parks: From the Back of the Bus to the Front of a Movement by Camilla Wilson (Scholastic, 2000)

Rosa Parks: My Story by Rosa Parks With James Haskins (Puffin, 1999)

The Year They Walked: Rosa Parks and the Montgomery Bus Boycott by Beatrice Siegel (Simon & Schuster, 1992)

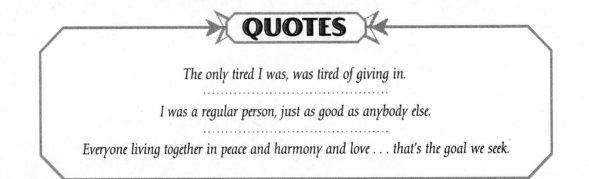

QUOTES

The only tired I was, was tired of giving in.

I was a regular person, just as good as anybody else.

Everyone living together in peace and harmony and love . . . that's the goal we seek.

Martin Luther King, Jr.
Dreams of Justice

by Adam Grant

Characters

Narrators 1 and 2

Martin Luther King, Jr.

Daddy, *Martin's father*

Mother, *Martin's mother*

Arthur, *Martin's first friend*

Mrs. Bradley, *Martin's teacher*

Bus Driver

Students 1–3

Coretta Scott King, *Martin's wife*

E. D. Nixon, *a civil rights leader*

Ralph Abernathy, *a civil rights leader*

Reporter

Judge

Neighbors 1 and 2

NARRATOR 1: On January 15, 1929, a boy is born to a middle-class black family in Atlanta, Georgia. He is named Martin Luther King, Jr.

NARRATOR 2: As soon as little Martin can talk, it is clear that he is smart and thoughtful. It is not yet clear that in his short lifetime he will change the world.

NARRATOR 1: Martin's first friend is a little white boy named Arthur. When the two boys turn six, they start school—at different schools. Martin is confused.

MARTIN: Mother, why don't Arthur and I go to the same school?

MOTHER: He goes to the white school. You go to the black school.

NARRATOR 2: But what comes next is even more confusing.

ARTHUR: My daddy says you and I can't play together anymore.

MARTIN: Why not?

ARTHUR: Because you're black and I'm white.

NARRATOR 1: Martin tells his parents what Arthur said.

MARTIN: Why would his daddy say that?

NARRATOR 2: Martin's parents look at each other.

MOTHER: Martin, honey, there are some things that you must begin to understand about our world.

DADDY: I wish we could have waited until you were older to have this discussion.

NARRATOR 1: That night, Martin's parents explain it all to him. Less than a hundred years ago, their people were slaves in the very city they live in. Many people in their community still discriminate against them because of the color of their skin.

DADDY:	Some of these white people will spend their last breath trying to make sure you don't enjoy the rights and privileges they do.
MOTHER:	Don't scare the boy.
DADDY:	He has to know the truth. He's not safe otherwise.
NARRATOR 2:	They tell Martin about the unfair Jim Crow laws, enacted to keep blacks and whites separate.
DADDY:	You must be careful not to use the white water fountains, washrooms, restaurants, and waiting rooms.
NARRATOR 1:	They tell Martin about lynchings, and terrorists called the Ku Klux Klan. Soon, Martin's head is spinning. Finally, his mother leans in close to him.
MOTHER:	Listen to me carefully, Martin. These unfair laws, these messages of hate, are meant to do only one thing: make you feel like you're not as good as other people.
NARRATOR 2:	Martin listens to her words.
MOTHER:	You must not let that happen. You must always remember, God made you just as good as anyone else. You got that?
MARTIN:	Yes, Mother.

SCENE 2

NARRATOR 1:	When Martin is fourteen, he enters and wins a debate contest in a nearby town.
NARRATOR 2:	Afterwards, he and his teacher, Mrs. Bradley, board the bus for the long ride home.
NARRATOR 1:	Soon the bus is crowded and still more passengers are getting on. Martin sees the driver looking at him in the rearview mirror.
BUS DRIVER:	Don't just sit there. Get up! These two white people need seats— you two better move to the back where you belong.

NARRATOR 2:	Martin does not move. The driver curses him.
BUS DRIVER:	I can send you to jail for this!
MRS. BRADLEY:	Martin, I know this is humiliating, but will you move for my sake?
NARRATOR 1:	Finally, Martin agrees to give up his seat. He and Mrs. Bradley stand for the ninety-mile journey home. Later, Martin writes these words in his autobiography:
MARTIN:	That night will never leave my memory. It was the angriest I have ever been in my life.
NARRATOR 2:	That summer, Martin travels to Connecticut to work on a tobacco farm. He is shocked by the different way of life in the north. He writes his father a letter:
MARTIN:	On our way here we saw some things I had never [expected] to see. After we passed Washington, there was no discrimination at all. The white people here are very nice. We go to any place we want to and sit anywhere we want to.
NARRATOR 1:	When he returns home, Martin is heartbroken by the way Southern black people still suffer from oppression.
MARTIN:	One day I'm going to help my people. But how?

≫ SCENE 3 ≪

NARRATOR 2:	Martin enrolls in a college when he is only fifteen. After graduation, he decides to become a minister like his father. He goes up north to study for his master's degree and Ph.D.
NARRATOR 1:	His life changes when he sees a lecture on the life of Mohandas K. Gandhi. Martin and his fellow students spend hours talking about him.

MARTIN: What do we know about Gandhi? He was a native Indian when India was a British colony. He wanted to find a way to free India from the British.

STUDENT 1: Gandhi knew that his poor and oppressed people didn't stand a chance against the terrifying British army. The only way to defeat them was through nonviolent protest.

STUDENT 2: So he began organizing sit-ins and boycotts against the British government. He went on hunger strikes. He and his fellow protesters were beaten and jailed by the British. But he tried to make sure that they never fought back.

STUDENT 3: Eventually, with the whole world watching, the British were shamed into giving India her independence.

MARTIN: How did Gandhi convince his people not to fight?

STUDENT 1: He said that the greatest power on earth was love and belief in justice. He called this Satyagraha (Sot-ya-GRAH-ha), which means "soul force."

STUDENT 2: The idea is to refuse to cooperate with an evil system. The forces of evil cannot stand against the forces of love.

NARRATOR 2: A light bulb goes on in Martin's head.

MARTIN: That's exactly what Jesus preached. Love your enemy. Violence only begets violence.

NARRATOR 1: Suddenly, Martin knows how he can help his people.

MARTIN: Nonviolent resistance. The chain of hatred must be cut. When it is broken, brotherhood can begin.

SCENE 4

NARRATOR 2: In 1955, Martin earns his graduate degree. He gets married. He and his new wife, Coretta, move to Montgomery, Alabama, where he takes a job as a Baptist minister.

NARRATOR 1:	At the time, Montgomery is a very segregated city. It is run by a racist white government, with terrible Jim Crow laws. For instance, blacks are only allowed to sit in the back of buses. And even in the back, they must give up their seats to whites if there are no other seats.
NARRATOR 2:	One day on a crowed Montgomery bus, a brave black woman named Rosa Parks refuses to give up her seat to a white man. She is arrested and thrown in jail.
NARRATOR 1:	Martin is in his office when his friend E. D. Nixon calls to tell him about the arrest.
NIXON:	Martin, we have taken this treatment for too long. Mrs. Parks is going to challenge her conviction in court. But that's not enough. We must take action. It's time to boycott the buses.
NARRATOR 2:	Martin realizes he must now put his theories of nonviolence to the test. He is elected president of the boycott committee. A few nights later, he leads a mass meeting to kick off the boycott.
MARTIN:	We are here this evening to say to those who have mistreated us so long that we are tired—tired of being segregated and humiliated, tired of being kicked about by the brutal feet of oppression.
NARRATOR 1:	Martin reminds the spellbound crowd how important it is to remain nonviolent during the boycott. Then he wraps up his speech.
MARTIN:	If we protest courageously, and yet with dignity and Christian love, when the history books are written in the future, somebody will have to say, there lived a race of people, of black people, of people who had the moral courage to stand up for their rights. And thereby they injected a new meaning into the veins of history and civilization.

NARRATOR 2: The boycott is off to a great start. Almost all of Montgomery's black citizens stay off the buses. But it's difficult. People soon grow tired of walking long distances to work.

NARRATOR 1: Car pools are started. And black taxi companies charge only the bus fare to drive boycotters to work. But still, most people have to walk.

NARRATOR 2: Martin speaks at meetings twice a week to inspire the troops.

MARTIN: Our campaign is not against individuals, but against the forces of evil in the world. And if there is a victory, it will be a victory not merely for fifty thousand black people, but a victory for justice and the forces of light!

NARRATOR 1: At one meeting, Martin gets an urgent message.

NIXON: Martin, your house has been bombed!

NARRATOR 2: Martin rushes home. There is a huge crowd on his lawn. The porch has been blown off his house.

MARTIN: Where are my wife and baby?

CORETTA: We're right here, Martin. We're both safe.

NARRATOR 1: A large crowd of black neighbors gathers outside, furious that someone tried to kill their leader. Some of them have guns.

NEIGHBOR 1: Where is Dr. King?

NEIGHBOR 2: I want to know who did this to Dr. King!

NARRATOR 2: Finally, Martin realizes that only he can keep this from turning into a riot. He goes outside and holds his hands up to quiet the crowd.

MARTIN:	My wife and baby are all right. I want you to go home and put away your weapons. We cannot solve this problem through violence. We must meet hate with love.
NARRATOR 1:	Finally, the crowd leaves peacefully.

SCENE 6

NARRATOR 2:	The boycott drags on for nearly a year. The national news media cover it heavily, and make Martin a star.
NARRATOR 1:	Anti-black violence rises. Martin himself receives up to forty death threats a day. But the boycotters remain nonviolent.
NARRATOR 2:	Soon, Martin's close friend, Ralph Abernathy, tells him of another problem.
ABERNATHY:	The city is claiming that our car pools are illegal. They may be able to shut them down.
NARRATOR 1:	That night at dinner, Martin talks sadly to Coretta.
MARTIN:	If they stop the carpooling, we're done. Our people have been suffering through this boycott for almost a year. How can I tell them it just got harder? I'm afraid it might be over.
CORETTA:	Martin, as long as I've known you, you've been able to do the impossible. Somehow, you'll do it again. I know it.
NARRATOR 2:	On November 13, 1956, almost a year after the boycott began, Martin is in court for the judge's ruling on the car pool.
JUDGE:	This court hereby finds in favor of the city. The illegal car pool is ordered to shut down. And the protest group is ordered to pay a fine of $15,000.
NARRATOR 1:	Martin is in despair. It is all over. But moments later, an amazing thing happens. Martin is approached by a reporter.
REPORTER:	Did you hear? The Supreme Court has struck down the Montgomery bus segregation law!

NARRATOR 2: During the boycott, Rosa Parks and her lawyers had fought her arrest and conviction all the way to the U.S. Supreme Court. Now, the Court has ruled that the Montgomery bus segregation law is against the Constitution. Martin and the Montgomery boycotters have won.

NARRATOR 1: That night, a huge crowd assembles at Martin's church. They scream and cheer as he takes the podium.

MARTIN: We must not take this as victory over the white man, but as a victory for justice and democracy. In the past, we have sat in the back of the buses, and this has indicated a basic lack of self-respect. It shows that we have thought of ourselves as less than men. On the other hand, the white people have sat in the front and thought of themselves as superior. Both approaches are wrong. Our duty is going back on the buses is to destroy this superior-inferior relationship. It is our duty to act in the manner best designed to establish man's oneness.

EPILOGUE

NARRATOR 2: Through his nonviolence resistance movement, Dr. Martin Luther King, Jr., went on to lead and win most of the major battles of the civil rights movement. In 1964, he won the Nobel Prize for Peace. He was arguably the most important American of the twentieth century.

NARRATOR 1: King's "I Have a Dream" speech, given at the 1963 March on Washington, is one of the most beloved speeches in American history.

NARRATOR 2: King was killed by an assassin's bullet on April 4, 1968, in Memphis, Tennessee. He was only thirty-nine years old.

Martin Luther King, Jr.

Background

Martin Luther King, Jr., was born on January 15, 1929, in Atlanta, Georgia. He graduated from Morehouse College in 1948, and was ordained as a Baptist minister. While studying theology at Crozer Seminary in Chester, Pennsylvania, King attended a lecture on Mohandas Gandhi's nonviolent struggle for freedom for the people of India. Gandhi's teachings had a profound effect on the young Baptist minister. Upon graduation, King received a scholarship to pursue a doctoral degree at Boston University. There he met Coretta Scott, who was studying voice at the Boston Conservatory of Music. The two were married in 1953. They had four children.

King's involvement in nonviolent protest began in 1955, in Montgomery, Alabama, where he led a successful boycott of the city's buses. Over the next 13 years, he promoted nonviolence as a means for African Americans to achieve their civil rights, and he was jailed several times. King also helped found the Southern Christian Leadership Conference (SCLC) in 1957. Internationally, he was viewed as an eloquent and forceful proponent of nonviolence. Among other prizes and awards given to him, King was honored with the Nobel Peace Prize in 1964. Four years later, at the age of 39, he was assassinated in Memphis, Tennessee. Today, King's birthday, January 15, is celebrated as a national holiday.

For Discussion

A NONVIOLENT SOLUTION

Conflicts arise among people almost every day. Some are minor; others are more serious. Discuss possible sources of conflict between individuals or groups of people. Make a list of the situations that students generate. Then have pairs of students role-play the conflicts and the solutions. How many different nonviolent resolutions do students create?

WE HAVE DREAMS, TOO

Read aloud the entire text of the "I Have a Dream" speech that King delivered in Washington, D.C., or have students take turns reading it aloud. What are the students' dreams for America? Discuss what they think can be done to make their dreams come true.

YOUNG LEADER

Dr. King was only 26 years old when he took leadership of the Montgomery bus boycott. Ask students what they think are the advantages and disadvantages of being a young leader. Explore with them their thoughts on what the minimum age one must be to be considered a leader. Have them explain their answers.

Write About It

ANOTHER MAN OF PEACE

The teachings of Mohandas K. Gandhi influenced Martin Luther King, Jr., and had a direct impact on the civil rights movement in America. Ask students to work in groups of three or four to research Gandhi's life and words and the struggle for Indian independence from England. Have them use the research to write a play about Gandhi.

IN HONOR OF DR. KING

Many communities in the United States have named streets or buildings in honor of Martin Luther King, Jr. Have students select a public place such as a park, an airport, or a town square in which to commemorate Dr. King. They should design a statue or monument that pays tribute to the civil rights leader's achievements. Let the students present their drawings or models along with maps showing the sites they propose to the rest of the class, along with a paragraph of key information to add as an inscription.

CARRYING ON A TRADITION

Although Coretta Scott was from Alabama, she met Martin Luther King, Jr., in Boston, where she was studying to become a singer. Her plans changed. She married King, and they had a family. Coretta accompanied her husband to India, endured threats and bombings, and participated in the civil rights movement. Urge students to discover more about her life. Have them create a television documentary focusing on Coretta Scott King's life. They may incorporate photographs, quotes, and maps into their script.

Additional Reading

Dare to Dream: Coretta Scott King and the Civil Rights Movement by Angela Shelf Medearis (Puffin, 1999)

King: A Photobiography of Martin Luther King, Jr. by Charles Johnson (Viking Penguin, 2000)

. . . If You Lived at the Time of Martin Luther King by Ellen Levine (Scholastic, 1990)

QUOTES

Nonviolent resistance is not a method for cowards; it does resist. If one uses this method because he is afraid or merely because he lacks the instrument of violence, he is not truly nonviolent.

Any law that uplifts human personality is just. Any law that degrades human personality is unjust. All segregation statutes are unjust because segregation distorts the soul and damages the personality.

We mustn't lose faith. Love will triumph over hate.

Shirley Chisholm
Unbought and Unbossed

by Kathleen Conkey

 ## Characters

Narrators 1 and 2

Emmeline Seales,
*Shirley's
grandmother*

Odessa,
Shirley's sister

Muriel,
Shirley's sister

Shirley Chisholm

Louis Warsoff,
*Professor at Brooklyn
College*

Wesley Holder,
*Head of Bedford-
Stuyvesant Political
League*

John McCormack,
*Speaker of the House
of Representatives*

Wilbur Mills,
*U.S. Representative
from Arkansas*

College Students 1–3

SCENE 1

NARRATOR 1: The year is 1934. A ten-year-old girl, who will one day be known throughout the world as Shirley Chisholm, is preparing to make a long journey from the Caribbean island of Barbados to New York City. Shirley, Odessa, and Muriel St. Hill have lived with their grandmother Emmaline Seales in Barbados for seven years.

NARRATOR 2: When Shirley was three, her parents, who had immigrated to America, brought the girls to stay with their grandmother in Barbados. At that time, the St. Hills couldn't give their daughters a good home in New York. But Mr. St. Hill had gotten a job at a burlap factory, and his wife worked as a seamstress. Mrs. St. Hill was coming soon to take her daughters back home to New York.

EMMELINE: (*Shirley's grandmother and two sisters sit on the porch.*) Shirley, if you don't come out here right this minute, we'll be late! What will your mama think?

ODESSA: Hurry!

SHIRLEY: (*stepping out onto the porch*) I don't want to go to New York City. It's smoky and dirty and noisy and cold. I want to stay here with you, Granny, where it's warm and your cooking is so sweet.

EMMELINE: Your mama and papa have been working their fingers to the bone so they could take you girls home! Now you say you don't want to go?

SHIRLEY: What took them so long?

MURIEL: Yeah, what took them so long?

EMMELINE: Girls, they didn't have a choice. How could they both work so hard and take care of three little girls at the same time? They brought you here because they love you. And it's been my blessing to take care of you.

SHIRLEY: It's not fair that some women can't work and keep their children, too. When I grow up I'm going to be a teacher and keep my family right beside me.

EMMELINE: You're a smart girl, Shirley. If you put your mind to something, it gets done. But what you're talking about means changing the whole world.

SHIRLEY: I can do that.

EMMELINE: Oh, child, I believe you just might, but right now we've got to go and meet your mama's boat.

SCENE 2

NARRATOR 1: The year is 1946. Shirley Chisholm is a young woman now. She's about to graduate from Brooklyn College. In high school, Shirley's grades were so high that four colleges offered her scholarships. She chose Brooklyn College so she could stay close to her family.

NARRATOR 2: In college, Shirley studied sociology because she was concerned about relations between blacks and whites and between rich and poor. She also found out that she loved to argue. Shirley was such a persuasive speaker that she was selected to be captain of the College Debating Society.

SHIRLEY: *(In a classroom at Brooklyn College, Shirley and another student are practicing for a debate.)* In conclusion, I remind you that all the facts, all the sociological evidence, and indeed, the moral compass inside the heart and soul of each of us, make clear that every child, whether white or black, rich or poor, deserves a good education and the opportunity to attend college. *(The students and Professor Warsoff applaud.)*

STUDENT 1: That was great, Shirley. I'm sure we're going to win.

SHIRLEY: Thank you. It should be a good contest.

WARSOFF:	*(approaching Shirley, as the students leave)* You're quite a public speaker, Miss St. Hill. Have you thought about what to do when you graduate in June? I hope you've settled on something that will make use of your debating skills.
SHIRLEY:	I'm going to teach young children.
WARSOFF:	Ah. I'm sure you'll make a fine teacher, but . . . you have so much fire in you—will teaching really hold your attention?
SHIRLEY:	Professor Warsoff, surely you agree it's one of the greatest things an adult can do for a child?
WARSOFF:	You have me there, Miss St. Hill. Still . . . another great thing you could do is to go into politics. Think of all the people you could help then.
SHIRLEY:	Politics?! Professor, how many black women do you know of in politics?
WARSOFF:	None, but . . .
SHIRLEY:	But you think Shirley St. Hill of Brooklyn, New York, can be the first?
WARSOFF:	Yes, I do. Why not involve yourself at the local level? Learn the ropes and then run for local office? Just give it some thought.

SCENE 3

NARRATOR 1:	After graduating from Brooklyn College, Shirley taught nursery school during the day. At night, she took classes at Columbia University and received her master's degree in education.
NARRATOR 2:	It wasn't long before Shirley was named as director of a day care center. She was in charge of more than one hundred fifty children and a staff of teachers and social workers. She also had time to get married to Conrad Chisholm, too! Then something happened that made Shirley Chisholm jump into politics.

SHIRLEY:	*(entering the offices of the Bedford-Stuyvesant Political League)* I'd like to speak to the person in charge, please.
WESLEY:	That would be me. I'm Wesley Holder. *(offering his hand, the two shake)*
SHIRLEY:	I'm Shirley Chisholm. I'd like to do what I can to help Lewis Flagg get elected judge.
WESLEY:	We can always use help here at the League. Why don't you tell me a little about yourself?
SHIRLEY:	I'm the director of the Hamilton-Madison Day Care Center in Manhattan, but I live here in Brooklyn. I've lived here almost all my life. I don't think a lawyer who lives in Manhattan should be elected to be a judge in a community he doesn't know anything about.
WESLEY:	The Democratic political bosses here in Brooklyn are the ones who asked the Manhattan lawyer to run here. If you work here for Lewis Flagg, you'll be going against them. They're pretty powerful men.
SHIRLEY:	Exactly—that's why I'm here: to help Lewis Flag get elected.
WESLEY:	*(smiling)* When can you start?
SHIRLEY:	I already have.

SCENE 4

NARRATOR 1:	Lewis Flagg was elected. Shirley remained politically active. Professionally, she continued to rise in the ranks. New York City appointed her its chief educational consultant for its day nurseries. In 1964, Shirley ran for the New York State Assembly and won. She was the first African-American woman ever elected to office in Brooklyn.

NARRATOR 2: Shirley Chisholm continued to add "firsts" to her list. In 1968, she ran and won a place in the U.S. House of Representatives. Her campaign slogan was "Unbought and Unbossed." Soon, Shirley was holding her own against the powerful Democrat who handed out committee assignments to new representatives from his party–the Speaker of the House.

McCORMACK: *(in the office of John McCormack, Speaker of the House of Representatives in Washington, D.C., 1969)* I understand that you're upset about the committee you've been put on. Here's the situation: First-year representatives never get appointed to the committees they want to be on. Be a good soldier, Mrs. Chisholm.

SHIRLEY: I'm not a soldier, Mr. Speaker. I'm a representative from one of the largest cities in the world, with years of experience inside our schools. Doesn't it make more sense for me to be on the Education Committee, which I asked for, instead of being on the House Agricultural Committee? That's ridiculous! I don't know anything about trees.

McCORMACK: Then you'll be learning a lot, Mrs. Chisholm. Show your constituents back home what a good learner you are. In a couple of years, we'll see about getting you on the Education Committee.

SHIRLEY: My constituents do not live in rural villages, they live in Brooklyn. There are no forests in Brooklyn. Brooklyn has schools . . .

McCORMACK: Then think of me as your teacher, and do what I tell you to do. Be a good soldier.

SCENE 5

SHIRLEY: *(a short time later in a meeting of the House Democrats)* Mr. Mills, I want you to withdraw my name from the House Agricultural Committee.

MR. MILLS: You can't do that.

SHIRLEY: I will serve the people of my district, and the people of the United States, better on the Education Committee.

MILLS: I will give you one more chance, Mrs. Chisholm. Will you withdraw your request?

SHIRLEY: *(firmly)* No, sir.

NARRATOR 1: Shirley Chisholm and Wilbur Mills stare at each other without saying a word. The other Democrats in the room can't believe what they're seeing and hearing. A week later Shirley is reassigned to the Veterans Affairs Committee. "At least," she said, "there are veterans in Brooklyn. And there is a Veterans Administration Hospital there, too."

EPILOGUE

NARRATOR 2: After serving in Congress for fourteen years, Shirley Chisholm ran for President—the first woman and the first African American ever to run. Although she didn't win the 1972 race, she paved the way for others—Geraldine Ferraro, who ran for vice president in 1984, and Jesse Jackson, who ran for president in 1984 and 1988. More importantly, Shirley Chisholm never let anyone tell her she couldn't achieve exactly what she wanted. She truly was "Unbought and Unbossed."

Shirley Chisholm

Background

Shirley Chisholm was born Shirley St. Hill in Brooklyn, New York, in 1924, to parents who had emigrated from the West Indies. After graduating from Brooklyn College with a degree in sociology in 1946, she attended night school at Columbia University for her master's degree in education. There Shirley met her first husband, Conrad Chisholm, whom she married in 1949 (and divorced in 1977). Chisholm's teaching career began at Mt. Calvary Child Care Center in Harlem. In 1953, she was appointed director of Friends' Day Nursery in Brooklyn; in 1959, she joined the New York City Division of Day Care and eventually became chief educational consultant.

Politically active in college, Chisholm went on to participate in politics in her community. In 1953, she became associated with the Bedford-Stuyvesant Political League; in the early '60s she helped form the Unity Democratic Club, an important black political club in Brooklyn. Chisholm ran for State Assembly in 1964, where she served two terms. She won a Congressional seat in 1968, becoming the first African-American woman in Congress. While in Congress she helped found the Congressional Black Caucus. Although she didn't win in 1972, Chisholm's historic run for President helped galvanize the budding women's movement. After retiring from Congress in 1982, she taught political courses at Mount Holyoke College and became chair of the National Political Caucus of Black Women. Today, Shirley Chisholm remains an active and outspoken supporter of women's and African-American rights.

For Discussion

AUTHORITY FIGURES

Shirley Chisholm was famous for questioning authority. For instance, she once joined in a boycott of President Nixon's State of the Union address after he refused to meet with members of the Congressional Black Caucus. Ask students if they've ever wanted to say "no" to authority figures. Did they do it? If so, what happened? If not, why didn't they? You may wish to share your own experiences as an authority figure who has been challenged.

THAT'S DEBATABLE

Shirley Chisholm loved to debate. In college, she argued such topics as whether or not 18-year-olds should be given the right to vote, and the pros and cons of capital punishment. Randomly divide the class into two groups, the pros and the cons. Throw out a current topic and let the two groups debate it. Before beginning the debate, each group should meet to discuss its strategy. Afterwards, discuss students' individual feelings about the topic.

WHERE WERE YOU?—AN ORAL HISTORY

Since the protests of the civil rights movement occurred in relatively recent history, chances are that students know people who were involved in some way, or remember the time well. As a class, brainstorm questions they have about the period of the 1950s, 1960s, and 1970s. Together, draw up a series of interview questions to ask family, friends, teachers, or any other willing participants. Depending on availability of equipment, students may be able to record their interviews. Otherwise, students and interviewees might work together in writing down responses. Have students present their findings (along with any possible artifacts) to the class.

Write About It

WHO SPEAKS FOR US?

Shirley Chisholm was the first African-American woman elected to the U.S. Congress. What is the makeup by ethnicity and gender of the U.S. Congress today? How does the class population compare to that of the Senate or House of Representatives? To begin the activity, have students make two circle graphs—one should show the ethnic breakdown of the class and the other should show the breakdown by gender. Then they should create circle graphs that show the ethnicity and gender of the Congress.

A BILL'S OWN LIFE

Nine of the bills that Shirley Chisholm introduced to the New York State Assembly passed. Which issues most concern your students? What would they like to see changed in our society? Suggest that students draft bills addressing their concerns. Then they can circulate their bills to their classmates and try to win support. What kinds of compromises are they willing to make to get their bills passed? How do their final versions compare to their first drafts? Students should present the final versions of their bills to the rest of the class for a vote.

EDUCATION AND MORE

Shirley Chisholm had a particular interest in education that didn't stop when she got to Washington, D.C. Divide the class into groups and have each group research civil rights developments in one area such as employment, housing, or voting, as well as sports, education, and so on. Then have each group present an oral report.

Additional Reading

Black Civil Rights Champions by Kimberly Hayes Taylor (Oliver Press, 1995)

Famous Firsts of Black Women by Martha Ward Plowden (Pelican, 2002)

Women of the U.S. Congress by Isobel V. Morin (Oliver Press, 1997)

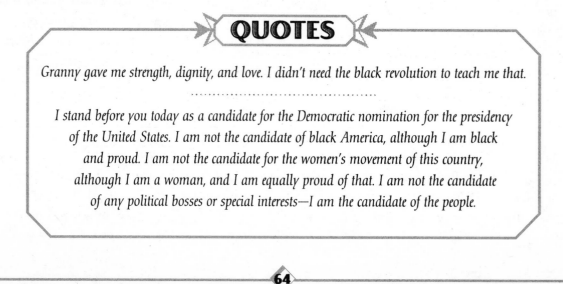

QUOTES

Granny gave me strength, dignity, and love. I didn't need the black revolution to teach me that.

. . . .

I stand before you today as a candidate for the Democratic nomination for the presidency of the United States. I am not the candidate of black America, although I am black and proud. I am not the candidate for the women's movement of this country, although I am a woman, and I am equally proud of that. I am not the candidate of any political bosses or special interests—I am the candidate of the people.